T0128904

FOREVER FRIENDS

THROUGH THICK AND THIN AND THE END

ELEANOR MILLER

FOREVER FRIENDS
THROUGH THICK AND THIN AND THE END

iUniverse books may be ordered through booksellers or by contacting:

iUniverse
1663 Liberty Drive
Bloomington, IN 47403
www.iuniverse.com
1-800-Authors (1-800-288-4677)

ISBN: 978-1-5320-3903-4 (sc)
ISBN: 978-1-5320-3904-1 (e)

Print information available on the last page.

iUniverse rev. date: 12/13/2017

A Friend

The dictionary online defines a friend as being a person whom one knows and with whom one has a bond of mutual affection, typically exclusive of sexual or family relations.

But then there are persons who can be classified as a "True friend".

A True Friend is someone who knows everything there is to know about you, and still calls you their friend. Someone who has seen you at your worst and did not judge you or belittle you.

A True Friend is one who will be there through thick and thin, they will be there to the end.

CONTENTS

A Collection of Poetry for Comfort while Grieving

PREFACE

Have you ever wondered how a friendship begins? As you reflect on some of the persons who entered your life and later became a friend, pause and think how it all got started. Was it fate, coincidental, or by divine intervention? After giving it some thought, I'm sure you will discover that a friendship can begin in various ways. Some of the most unexpected encounters, can turn out to produce a lasting friendship. For instance a conversation with someone you meet on the street, giving advice on how to prepare a certain food to someone in the super market, a word of encouragement at a church function, or a smile to a stranger at a party: any one of these chance meetings may start out with a simple conversation, then you soon discover that each of you have so much in common and before you know it a friendship has evolved.

Then there are friendships that develop early in life as early as during a person's kindergarten years. Those are the friendships that have proven to be the longer lasting ones. They somehow manage to continue through elementary, high school, college, and even for as long as each individual lives.

Those kindergarten years are the most impressionable years. They are the times when children are so innocent and carefree. At that time in life children aren't influenced as to who their friends are by such things as the color of one's skin, who one another's parents are, or how big or small the house one resides in. All these kids know at that age is they like being around each other and when they are apart there is a feeling of emptiness and sadness.

I remember reading an excerpt on the life of Dorothy Height, (March 24 1912- April 20 2010), an African American woman who wore many hats in every sense that the word implies. In the literal sense, she loved wearing her fancy hats and one rarely saw her in public when she wasn't wearing one. Seeing pictures of Dorothy in her various hats reminds me of the queen of England: how elegant she looked, just like royalty. She also wore many hats meaning she held many titles in life, among them being an Educator, Civil Rights Activist, President of the Negro Council of Women and others.

In this excerpt Dorothy tells of becoming friends with a White child in her neighborhood of Rankin Pennsylvania, when her family first moved there. She recounts how one day when she went to play with her friend, the White child said she could no longer be her friend. When Dorothy asked why, the White child responded "because you are Colored." We know that this attitude did not originate with the child but from someone else who had an influence in the child's life, perhaps her parents. Children do not look at the differences that exist among one another they simply look at the things that unite them. If all of people could look at the qualities that exist among individuals which unites them, oh what a wonderful and peaceful world this would be.

How devastated Dorothy and her friend must have been for each had missed an opportunity to develop a lasting friendship. The color of a person's skin should not be a barrier when it comes to determining who one can be friends with.

As friends at kindergarten age, you play together, you eat together, you hug and kiss each other, you share, all because you are friends and that is what friends do. Do you sometimes reflect on some of the friends you had when you were a child? I do, and thinking about them I realize that some of the things we did and the things we said showed how innocent we were. As time passed and we matured, we know now that we were just being kids. We were just friends.

The friendships which begin early in life usually follow you all through your school years and even when each have graduated and gone their separate ways, you still remember that person as your friend. A phone call, postcard, letter or an e- mail rekindles the memories of the past, and it is as if you never separated. Have you ever longed for those care-free days again? I'm sure your answer is yes, because I must admit I certainly have. I realize just how fortunate it is to be able to address someone as friend. I'm not talking about just a friend, but a true friend, one who will stick by you no matter what.

I can recall having several persons that were considered to be my friends when I was attending elementary school. There was one person in particular that I chose to call my very best friend. As I reflect on that childhood friend, there were times when we were at odds with one another, but in the end, we remained friends.

That's the beauty of a true friend. You both can disagree and still remain friends.

When I see that friend's grown children, even now I say to them, "Your mother was my best friend in school." They respond, "I know". I don't know if their acknowledgement of this is because their mother addresses me as such or because of the many times I have reiterated it to them. I spent so many Sunday afternoons at her house and she at mine. We had a friendship like non other. Although I rarely see her now, I still think of her as my friend. Those early days are forever etched in my memory.

Then there is another kind of friendship, a friendship that develops out of each individual's need for the other. That is what this book details, a friendship developed late in one individual's life and during unordinary circumstances, yet the friendship endured.

How unlikely that a friendship would exist among these two individuals because they were different in so many ways. There was a difference in age, personalities, and social status, but none of these differences kept the two from becoming and remaining friends.

Just like the friendships that exist among kindergarten kids, where differences does not alter the fact that you are friends, neither did the demographics of each of these person's social background or status in life matter.

It didn't matter that one friend lived in a brick house and the other a trailer. Nor did it matter that one friend wore the best clothes brought from the most expensive department stores and the other shopped at the thrift stores. It did not matter that one had a bank account and the other lived from payday to payday, none of these differences mattered because they were friends. True friendship does not set meaningless boundaries.

This book gives a chronological account of how these two individuals became friends. It tells of some of the good times and also some of the bad times that they experienced together. It tells how they remained friends throughout the struggles of one friend's illnesses and subsequent death.

Again just like the friendships that begin in kindergarten and continued through graduation from elementary, high school and even college, this story speaks of a graduation of sorts. It details the graduation of a friend's life on this side and her transitioning to life eternal. This book tells of the ups and downs, ins and outs that came before her transition, and how those hard times did not cause their friendship to falter or dwindle away, they only made their friendship stronger.

Woven into the pages of this book are poems and prayers that helped to strengthen and sustain one friend as she coped with the other friend's sickness and ultimate demise.

Although one friend is no longer here, she shall never be forgotten. True friends never leave each other. Although one friend may make their residence somewhere else, they shall forever remain a part of you, because true friends remain friends forever, if only in the heart.

In Loving Memory of My Friend

John 15:15 (KJV)

Greater love has no one than this, that one
lay down his life for his friends. You are My
friends if you do what I command you.
I no longer call you servants, because a servant
does not know his master's business. Instead, I have
called you friends, for everything that I learned
from my Father I have made known to you.

INTRODUCTION

As Jesus was preparing to leave the disciples and take his place sitting at the right hand of God the Father, he spoke these words to them "Greater love has no one than this, that one lay down his life for his friends". *John 15:14* Implicitly Jesus told his disciples that they were his friends if they did what he commanded them to do. Jesus went on to say that they would no longer be addressed as servants, because a servant is not privy to all that the master does. But because he had opened up to them his past, present and future plans for them and man-kind, He now considered them his friends.

Everything that Jesus had learned from His Father, the disciples now knew.

To be addressed as a friend of God is a great honor. The word friend in itself implies a special relationship and bond between individuals. The love that Jesus had for the disciples and all of us is expressed in his willingness to go to the cross, be crucified, die, be buried and raised to life again in order to redeem us from sin and reconcile us back to God. What love! What a Friend! He did this because of the love that He and His Father had for us.

It does not matter if you are Black or White or any other race of people; nor does it matter if you are young or old, or any other difference that exists among individuals, if you do what Jesus commands, you are his friend.

Each one of us need to be able to call Jesus our friend. We also need to have someone in our lives that we can address as our earthly friend. Someone we can share everything with, a "True Friend". Have you found such a person? I did and I want to share our story with you.

1

Unraveling the Mystery

It is Christmas Eve, 2013 and while so many people are going about their usual hustle and bustle; shopping, cooking, gift wrapping, you know the last minute Christmas stuff, I sit quietly by the bedside of a dear friend who seems to be transitioning from life on this side to the life beyond.

She has had a good life. As I write this, God allowed her to reach eighty six years of age. She not only lived the promised years of three score years and ten, but also lived the extended years that comes with reason of strength (psalms 90:10) and even beyond that.

She pretty much did for herself up until several years ago. She drove herself where she wanted to go, cooked not only for herself but for so many others, and worked in her yard during the spring and early summer; these were her favorite times of the year. The azalea bushes in full bloom brought her so much joy. She captured their beauty in numerous photos that fill her picture albums. How she enjoyed pulling those old albums out and admiring not only the azaleas, but all of her flowers. Back then she was a very independent lady.

But now as I watch her these last few days drift in and out of consciousness, sometimes appearing to be in a comatose state, it is hard to believe she is that same vibrant person that I became acquainted with years ago.

I've read that before a person dies they go back to being a child with little or no communication, consuming tidbits of food and a sip of water every once and a while, just sleeping most of the time. According to those experienced in palliative care, this is a way the body prepares itself for the inevitable. She is at that stage now, and it seems it came so quickly.

The word of God tells us that life is even a vapor that appears for a little time, and then vanishes away. (James 4:14). So while she lies in limbo I ask myself will it be today, tomorrow, the next day, weeks or months from now that the wind of time will blow causing the life of my dear friend to evaporate?

Nobody knows but God when she shall breathe her last breath, therefore I sit, pray, wait, all the while jotting down words that might bring comfort to me and ease the agony of not knowing when she will expire.

God has a way of speaking to his children when they are faced with the uncertainties of life. If we get in a quiet place and be still he will give us the assurance we need to make it through.

Here is what He said to me.

The waves of grief and sorrow Seems
more than you can bear.
Your heart is heavy, your tears are
many and great is your despair.
Just cast your cares upon God,
knowing that He cares for you.
God will help you bear your burdens
He will shield and protect you too.
And if the wind becomes too boisterous, and
the waves going against God's will
He will simply speak these soft words on your behalf
"Peace be still"

Words by Reverend Eleanor D. Miller
…the wind and the waves obey Him.
Luke 8:25 KJV

Peace be still are the words that Jesus spoke when He and the disciples were on a ship and a storm arose at sea. The disciples were so afraid and went to the lower part of the ship to wake up Jesus saying "do you not care that we are perishing?" Jesus got up and rebuked the wind and the storm ceased. Then He said to the disciples "O Ye of Little Faith."

Death can be compared to a raging storm, for its effects can be just as devastating. While in a storm you don't know what the outcome will be, you just have to wait it out; the same thing applies to life and death, ultimately both are in God's hands.

It is in troubling times such as these that we cling more and more to our Faith and trust the one who is able to bring us through the storms of life and death. Whether the storms are physical, mental, financial or spiritual, listen for God to say,

"Peace be still"

Prayer

Dear God at times like these I rely on the three O's that represent your character to keep me strong and focused. You are *omniscient*, you know everything. You are *omnipresent*, everywhere at the same time. You are *omnipotent,* able to do anything because you are all powerful, you are the Almighty. Knowing this allows me to put my faith and my trust in you believing that you will work everything out for the good of all concerned. Let me hear you say "Peace Be Still" calming this storm that is raging in my life right now. In the blessed name of your son Jesus, the Christ I pray.

Amen

Personal Reflections

As you meditate on the goodness of God, can you remember the times that he showed you the 3Os that represent his character? If so write them down. Remembering will give you the reassurance you need to make it through this turbulent time in your life. Know that if He did it once, He will do it again. God never changes. He is the same yesterday, today, and forever.

_____

_____

_____

_____

_____

_____

_____

_____

_____

_____

Now thank God for reminding you of who He is! He is the one who is able to quiet the storms that are raging in your life right now.

There is a hymn written By William Cowper, and today looking upon the frail body of my friend, my mind takes me back to the first verse of that hymn. The poet says God moves in "a mysterious way. His wonders to perform; He plants His footsteps in the sea and rides upon the storm."

William Cowper was born in 1731 and died in the year 1800. After reading excerpts about Cowper's life, I can say he certainly had his share of storms. He had suffered bouts of depression which caused him to attempt suicide on several occasions. His suicide attempts were unsuccessful in the physical sense, but because of them and his struggles with depression, Cowper turned from Christianity. I feel that to give up on one's Faith causes a different kind of suicide, *spiritual suicide*. Cowper had survived the near drowning experience, the attempts of hanging himself, and even an attempt of poisoning himself but had come to a point in his spiritual life where he felt he was beyond redemption. He was still breathing, and doing all the things that suggests life, but he was dead inside because he had lost hope.

The dictionary defines *hope* as being the state which promotes the desire of positive outcomes related to events and circumstances in one's life or in the world at large. In other words, hope is telling oneself that no matter what it looks like, there is still a chance that things will turn around in a person's favor.

According to Hebrews 11:1 *Faith* is said to be the substance of things hoped for the evidence of things not seen. It is clear to me that if there is no faith, then there is no hope.

How can a person keep hope alive and hold on to their faith when circumstances suggest that there is nothing left to hope for? The answer can be found in *Lamentations 3:20-23*. The prophet Jeremiah writes "Surely my soul remembers and is bowed down within me. This I recall to my mind, therefore I have hope. The Lord's loving kindnesses indeed never cease, for His compassions never fail. They are new every morning; great is your faithfulness."

It is through remembering God our creator, and the love He has for His creation that we are able to cling to hope.. It is through knowing that God is faithful, (He will do what He says He will do), therefore, we look forward to pressing pass today and getting to the morning. No matter what things look like today, with morning comes new mercies, new grace and new opportunities. Remembering God's promises lets us find consolation in the fact that weeping may endure for the night, but joy comes in the morning. *Psalms 30:5*

As I stare at my friend I wonder what morning will bring for her. Will it be another day of lying in silence, with no strength or ability to even turn her head? Or will morning bring a miracle that will awaken her to a rejuvenated state where the past weeks would seem like a dream to her? The latter is what I hoped for. Then I thought that if morning should bring the inevitable, death, she would also awaken to a new life, only it would be an eternal life, a life everlasting. It would be a life without pain, suffering, agony, or all the struggles that life on this side can bring. It would be the life of peace and happiness, the life that Jesus came to give to all who believed in Him and who confess Him as their personal Savior.

Indeed the life lived by my friend was totally different from that of Cowper. She enjoyed life despite all the ups and downs she experienced. Whatever life threw at her she took it and managed to work her way through. She never lost hope. Her tenacity and determination can be attributed to her strong faith in God. Despite the pain that sometimes bought her to tears, she never once thought about ending her life.

On the nightstand beside her bed, lay a pistol she had kept for protection. There were several occasions in which the inclination came to me to remove it for thoughts of what she might do. You know all sorts of things go through a person's mind when they are suffering. However, my fear of guns would not allow me to touch it. As I write this, that pistol remains in the same exact spot where she left it.

Using that gun to end her suffering was a thought that never entered her mind. For when the pain seemed unbearable, she would cry out to the one who she believed could help, Jesus, her Savior. There were many instances when she would mutter "Lord have mercy" or "help me Jesus". There would be times when she would say "Lord what do you want me to do"? All of these utterances were audible prayers of a sort for God to help sustain her as she was dealing with whatever illness afflicting her body at that time. Those prayers and so many others were proof of her religious convictions.

I can recall coming to her bedroom door on numerous occasions when she was still at home to check on her because of the voices and noises she would be making.

When asked if she was alright, her reply would be "I'm okay, I'm just praying." The scripture says *Thou wilt keep him in perfect peace, whose mind is stayed on thee: because he trusteth in thee. Isaiah 25:3 NKJ* My friend trusted God wholeheartedly and prayed to him continually. Although her voice is silenced now, I know Jesus is still in her heart and she is still praying.

It's good that God knows our thoughts? Even now without uttering a single word, I know her mind is still on God, the one who knows everything. God knows when we sit down and when we rise up; He understand our thoughts from afar (**Psalms 139:2 NASB**). Because God knows, he will not put more on us than we can bear.

That's one of the scriptures I always reminded my friend of and her reply to me would be "that's right."

It was a perplexity as to why this particular hymn by Cowper had come to me, especially at this time. And even more perplexing was why my attention was drawn to a man who had lost his faith when my friend had held on to hers? Lord, I asked, what are you saying to me? I know everything that you do is done to teach us and to make us grow into more of the person you would have us be, but how can a man who lost his faith teach me anything? Right now I am in a pitiful state and I need something to increase my faith as I watch my friend slowly drift away. I don't need to be reminded of another's man's misery because right now I have more misery than I can seem to bear. Then I reminded myself that God knows just how much we can bear.

Still wondering and questioning God, it came to me that the hymn was originally titled **Conflict Light Shining out of Darkness** and was based on the scripture *John 13:7.* The original title of the song struck a chord with me, because several years ago I was inspired to write a book titled, **Let Your Light Shine.** The book was inspirational, and dealt with how Christians are the light of the world and should let their lights shine in every situation. (Matthew 5:14) Also in the book an analogy was made between candles and Christians. God had shown me that individuals who are Christians have an obligation to illuminate, shine into darkness, just like a candle.

Many times I've tried to be that light for my friend, never letting my true emotions show, but with each passing day this was getting harder to do. The months of watching my friend slowly decline were using up all of my spiritual energy: my light was beginning to flicker a sign that it was going out.

There was no need to remind me that to be absent from the body is to be present with the Lord (2nd Corinthian 5:8), and that flesh and blood cannot enter the kingdom of God (1st Corinthians 15:50). All of these scripture references were etched in my memory from the many times I had used them to comfort so many family and friends at the funeral of their loved ones. But regardless of how many times I had read or recited these scriptures those words did little to comfort me at this time. I knew that these scriptures were true, but in reality I wasn't ready to let my friend go.

Still searching for an answer as to the why of Cowper's hymn, immediately my bible, which was now my closet companion during these hard and troubling days of my dear friend's life, was turned to John 13:7. I needed something that would bring me back from the depressed state that I was experiencing, the kind of depression that accompanies the anticipated loss of a loved one. I wanted to see what revelation if any, would bring a bit of light to the darkness that was surrounding me.

God's word has a way of lifting the spirit.

In the scripture Jesus had humbled himself and washed the disciple's feet. No doubt the disciples really didn't understand His reasoning behind this. Here their Lord and soon to be Savior of the world had stooped down and washed their dirty feet. After finishing, Jesus then spoke to them saying "you will understand what I am doing later". Peter was adamant and said "Lord you shall never wash my feet". Jesus replied "if I don't wash your feet, you have no part in me". Jesus was teaching the disciples a lesson in humility, by setting an example for them to follow.

There are times when persons say things to us, and we don't fully grasp the meaning of what they are saying right away. Their comments may seem out of the ordinary, but as time goes by the revelation is made clear. This was the case with the disciples, eventually they would discover what Jesus meant. A couple of verses later in the scripture Jesus tells the disciples explicitly "if I being your Lord and Savior have washed your feet, you ought to wash one another feet."

In the scripture the implication went far beyond feet washing. Jesus wanted his disciples to know, you are to be there for one another and for others. You are to perform whatever duties are necessary to show that the love of Christ is in you.

Suddenly my mind became flooded with other scripture references; by this all men will know that you are my disciples if you love one another. (John 13:35) When you've done it to the least of these you have done it unto me. (Matthew 25:40) He that humbled himself shall be exalted and he that exalted himself shall be humbled. (Luke 14:11) Go ye therefore and teach all nations…(Matthew 28:19) The strong ought to bear the infirmities of the weak and not please ourselves (Romans 15:1).

Remembering these scriptures triggered another question. Lord I asked, haven't I done this for my friend? Could I, or should I have done more? Is this what you are saying to me; still no answer.

On numerous occasions I had washed my friend's feet when she became unable to bath herself. Carefully I would help her in the tub, and seat her on the bath chair. She was able to wash most of her body. After she had finished, I would do her back and her feet. If she could have done it herself, she would have, but I was more than delighted to do it for her. The gratitude she expressed to me for taking such care with her made me want to do even more.

Still unable to ascertain why Cowper and this particular hymn had come to me, once again my bible was opened and I reread John 13:7. It was after my second reading that it dawned on me why God had put the words to this hymn in my spirit. It wasn't about the hymn or about the writer, but about the latter part of the scripture reference, the part that reads *later you will understand.*

It wasn't the appropriate time for me to grasp all the mysteries that God had in store for me at this time. What I needed to do was to be there for my friend and let God's plan come to pass.

Softly the Spirit spoke to me and said "I know the plans I have for you… Trust Me"! How could I not trust God? He had never failed me in the past and I knew He knew better than I about what the future held for me and my friend.

2

The Beginning of A Friendship

My friend of more than ten years came into my life during the death of my dear mother. Mother went home to be with the Lord in August of 2001. This was a very sad and distressing time. Those of you who had experience the loss of a parent, especially your mother know how heart wrenching and difficult this can be.

So many times reflections on life at home flood my mind and recalling some of those memories caused me to acknowledge that mother was always there for us kids. It was late in her life that she began to work outside the home. During our childhood years she was always home with us, washing, cleaning, cooking, ironing, doing all the stuff that a good mother does for her children. She was indeed that virtuous woman as depicted in Proverbs 31:10. We, her children, did rise up, and call her blessed. Proverbs 31:28. Because she was blessed, we were blessed.

We didn't have much but we were thankful for what we had, mother taught us to always be thankful. I can not remember a time when we went without a meal. Our meals may not have consisted of the four and five course meals that most of us enjoy today, but we had food that sustained us from one day to the next.

Even after growing up and leaving home, we still looked forward to the gatherings at mother's house on holidays and special occasion. We relished the thought of mother pampering us the way she had done when we were kids. Nobody could cook like our mother, but isn't that the way all children feel about their mother?

Yes of course it is. Sadly all that is gone now but thank God for the memories.

It was the prayers of family and friends and those precious memories that made the pain of losing mother bearable. The sadness that filled my heart after the death of my mother was alleviated by some God inspired words of comfort. They helped me at that difficult time in my life so perhaps they will help me get through the sadness that I am experiencing now.

My dear friend had not succumbed to death as of yet. God had not taken her away from us in the physical, but mentally she was no longer with us, and in so many ways she was already gone. I would constantly tell myself that as long as she was breathing there was hope that she would recover. Yet with each day's passing I struggled to hold on to and cherish the past memories of us being together.

Our minds can sometime be a book that hold precious memories of the past. All we have to do is open the book, (our minds) to a certain time in life and the sad memories of the present seem to dissipate for a little while.

Memories

There's an emptiness in your heart
that only time can fill
The pain seems unbearable now,
but trust me God can heal.
Just tell God all about it,
the sadness and the pain
He'll lighten your burden
then you can laugh again.
Hold fast to your memories,
death didn't take them away
Live each moment to the fullest
and don't forget to pray
Prayer will make you stronger,
prayer will see you through
And always remember that
we are praying for you too.

Written by: Reverend Eleanor D. Miller

…but in everything by prayer and supplication, with thanksgiving, let your request be made known to God; and the peace of God, which surpasses all understanding will guard your hearts and minds through Christ Jesus.

Philippians 4:6, 7

Prayer

Dear God I pray that you grant me your peace, that surpasses all understanding. The peace that comes only from knowing you, and knowing that you never make a mistake. Knowing this I am able to surrender my will to your will. All our lives are in your hands, and there is no better hands to be in. In the name of Jesus I ask these things.

Amen

Personal Reflections

What do you need to surrender to God? Write them down for the scripture reminds us to cast all our cares upon Him, for He cares for us. 1st Peter 5:7

_____

_____

_____

_____

_____

_____

_____

_____

_____

_____

Doesn't it feel good to know that God cares for you? Now thank God for being a good listener.

Mothers' modest country home was packed with relatives and friends who came to offer condolences up until her burial. We laughed, we talked, we ate, and reminisced about so many things. It was wonderful to have so many of her family and friends to come and share with us at this time.

Out of all those who visited us, one particular person that came with tokens of sympathy is remembered with vivid detail. She was a beautiful, petite, brown skinned, well-dressed lady, whom I had seen on numerous occasions in passing. Her name, where she lived and who her relatives were, was no secret, for we were neighbors of sort, but there was not a personal connection between us. Perhaps our lack of social contact is what made the words she spoke to me that day so daunting and remained dormant in the inner recesses of my mind until now, just months prior to her demise.

That day this particular person handed me a card and a cake and after putting them away I returned to the living room where she was seated to fellowship. It was at that time that she leaned over and whispered "I'll be a mother for you" in my ear. Then she gave me one of the biggest smiles. Needless to say I did not understand her reason for saying this, and really didn't know how to reply, but courteously responded with a thank you.

Thinking to myself how could this woman whom I barely know be a mother to me? Did she know that being my mother would mean filling some mighty big shoes? Could she be that listening ear when I needed someone to talk to late in the mid night hour? Could she offer words of peace when my life was in turmoil and chaotic? Would she be able to reassure me that everything would be alright when it felt like the world was caving in all around me? These and so much more are the things that my mother was able to do.

Knowing that this woman had recently lost her husband, who had succumbed to death after a long period of declining health, I surmised that his death had left her saddened, alone, and in need of a friend.

I can recall her driving past my house going to visit her husband in the VA hospital before he passed. Every day she made the long drive up the mountain regardless if the weather was good or bad, she was faithful. So perhaps being a mother figure to me would somehow alleviate the loneliness that she was feeling. She had no children of her own and her step children lived miles and miles away. Maybe the words she spoke to me was her way of easing the pain that she had felt after her loss and she knew that same pain had to be enveloping me at the death of my mother.

So many times we have seen this scenario play out in the movies? You know the line people say to those who have suffered the loss of a loved one, "I'm sorry for your loss". Perhaps her comments to me, at that time were her way of saying just that, I'm sorry for your loss. She was only trying to shine some light into the darkness that death had brought.

To be honest the death of mother had darkened by blue sky, but I held on to the promise that God would never leave me or forsake me. His Son resides in the inside and He is the Light of the World. He is forever shining even during the darkest skies.

The "SON" Light

Although the sun is shining bright,
and there's not a cloud in the sky,
you are surrounded by darkness
because a loved one has said good-bye.
You wonder if things will lighten up again,
will the sun shine for you?
The answer is yes, in time;
because God will see you through.
God sent Jesus into the world
for the dark daysyou are going through;
And when the sun can't brighten your day
the **SON** will break through.

Words by Rev. Eleanor D. Miller
I have come as a light into the world, that whoever
believes in Me should not abide in darkness.
John 12:46

Prayer

Dear God thank you for your son Jesus. When we are experiencing dark days he is able to bring light. Also thank you for making it possible that we too can bring light to others if we have Jesus your SON in our hearts.

Amen

Personal Reflections

Has there ever been a time in your life when you had to bring light to a dark situation? Although you were experiencing gloom and sadness yourself, you managed to encourage someone else. Write down how you were able to make it through.

God's hands were on you and He gave you the strength to minister to those wo were suffering the same as you. You perhaps were a little bit stronger.

We then that are strong ought to bear the infirmities of the weak, and not please ourselves. Romans 15:1 (NIV)

Now thank God that you were able to let your light shine then, and this will allow you to see, that Jesus the Light of the World, dwells in you. You are not alone, even now.

That beautiful, brown skinned, petite, well-dressed-woman who uttered to me the words "I'll be a mother for you" that day, is the friend whose bedside I now sit by. Her age is shown by the wrinkles that are on her face, neck and hands. That petite frame has turned into almost skin and bones from the lack of an appetite and her refusal to eat. Her features are nothing like the woman that visited me so many years ago at mother's, but to me she is still just as beautiful, for her true beauty was not what showed on the outside but what was in her heart.

Not many people knew my friend the way I did. We shared some awesome times together and those times are dear to me and are locked in a special place, my heart.

A Special Place

That beautiful place that you shared
together is not special anymore
the one you shared it with is gone
never to return there, no more.
Hold on to the laughter you shared
in that special place;
Keep those memories close to you,
and never let them slip away,
One day when you are stronger
you can take a stroll down memory lane,
then you will discover the beauty
of that special place once again. The sound of
the birds chirping, the humming of the bee,
the smell of the honeysuckle
these memories will help to brighten your day.
No this sadness won't last forever,
it will gradually fade away.
You'll discover that although you and your loved
one are apart, they shall forever be with you,
for that special place that you shared
together, you shared it in your heart.

Words written by Rev. Eleanor D. Miller
*Give ear to my prayer, O God; and hide not
thyself from my supplication…My heart is sore
pained within me…Psalms 55:1, 4a.*

Prayer

Dear God I know that you do hear and answer prayer, therefore I cry out to You to ease the pain that my heart is feeling now. I know that Your Word says that one day you will wipe the tears from our eyes and that there will be no more sorrow. Help me to live so that when that blessed time comes, there will be a place for me in that New Heaven. In the name of Jesus, the Christ I pray.

Amen

Personal Reflections

Even when we do not have the words to say, God knows our thoughts from a far. Isaiah 65:24 says and it shall come to pass, that before they call, I will answer; and while they are yet speaking I will hear. Sometimes words aren't necessary, because God already knows. Write down if you have just thought about something and God knew and answered.

_____

_____

_____

_____

_____

_____

_____

_____

_____

_____

Why don't you thank Him for the unspoken prayers He has answered in the past.

Peering upon the frail body of my friend, the words written in 1st Samuel chapter 16 verse 7 comes to mind. God spoke these words to Samuel, *"Do not look at his appearance or his physical stature, because I have refused him; For the Lord does not see as man sees, for man looks at the outward appearance, but the Lord looks at the heart."*

Knowing that God looks at the heart made me confident that when we shall all stand before God to be judged, He will not refuse my friend a place in His blessed kingdom because He knew her heart. Although she sometimes could be abrupt, self-willed and stubborn, she had a heart after God's own heart. She was a giver and gave not only of her resources, but also of her time. Very few people knew the extent of her giving to others. Both family and friends and sometimes mere acquaintances benefitted from her giving heart.

What grieved me the most was the wondering of what would happen to me when that heart ceases to beat? Who will say to me now "I'm sorry for your loss" or better still, who will say I'll be a mother for you"? Who will shine the light into the darkness then?

As Jesus spoke to his disciples and said later you will understand, later for me is now, for the revelation had become clear about what my friend meant that day when she said "I'll be a mother for you". It was not so much about her being a mother for me, but about me being a daughter for her. I, like her, had suffered a loss and each one could fill the void that death had left in both of our lives. Sure I had brothers and sisters, husband and children, but there is nothing like a mother's love. She too had nieces and nephews, and as I mentioned earlier step children but nothing could compare to the inseparable love she and her husband had for each other. Now that an opportunity to give and receive love like a mother, would once again give purpose to her life. Yes this is what she longed for.

My mind focused was turned to the story of Hannah in the book of 1st Samuel. This story depicts the longing of a barren woman for children. Hannah loved her husband but was unable to give him children so he married another woman, Penninah who was able to have children. Penninah taunted Hannah and made life for her difficult because she was barren. When Hannah had taken all she could take, she prayed for God to give her a child. She vowed to give that child back to God. God answered her prayer and gave Hannah a son. She kept her vow to God and gave Samuel back to the Lord. God subsequently gave Hannah other children. Hannah now knew how being a mother felt. That void that she had felt for years had been filled by her giving birth.

God makes no mistakes and reflecting on the many hours, days, weeks, and years my friend and I spent together, I can say that my friend certainly lived up to the promise she made to me so many years ago. She was indeed that listening ear when I needed her to be. She had words to comfort me when I needed them, and just like a mother she had words that chasten me when it was needed also. Yes, she became a mother for me in every sense that the word implies. It is my hope that I lived up to what she expected me to be to her, a daughter. She didn't actually give birth to me but that's how we viewed our relationship. I loved her with the same unconditional love that I gave my birth mother.

A short while before her passing, my friend's mind began to slip, but every once and a while she remembered something that we did together, or something that we said to each other that let me know that with whatever was going on in her mind, she was still my friend. She would often say at times, "do you remember when... or do you remember that...?" As a matter of fact she was the one who brought back to my remembrance the mother statement. More than ten years had elapsed since my mother's passing and it was surprising to know that she was able to recollect what she had said to me that day. In her own words she said "I'll never forget that." At times she could not remember what happened in the last hour, but remembered with vivid details things that transpired years ago. I'm so glad she remembered that statement, and brought it back to my attention, for it puts everything in perspective now.

Cowper was right in his hymn, God indeed moves in mysterious ways, because I don't even know how our friendship developed, but looking back I do know that it was all in God's plan. The words of **Jeremiah 29:11** reads, *for I know the plans I have for you," declares the Lord, "plans to prosper you and not to harm you, plans to give you hope and a future.* But the question that often came to me is what would my future be without my friend? I dreaded the thought of not being able to talk to her or see her. Then it dawned on me I shall see her on the other side, for eternal life was what she had striven for in her later years and it is what I too am striving for.

I've often said that we can only see the here and now, but God sees further on down the road. He looked down through time and he saw the things that would transpire in my friend's life before he called her home. So he put the wheels in motion to insure that someone would be there for her. I'm thankful that someone was me.

3

Taking the Friendship to a Different Level

Mother had been gone for months now and life was getting back to normal. One day out of nowhere I got a call inviting me to lunch, I accepted the invitation coming from the husband and wife ministry team. We agreed on a time and when they arrived to pick me up who was with them, none other than the lady that had visited me after mother's passing. She was seated in the back and when my eyes caught hers, that same vibrant smile that she gave me that day at mother's house came across her face.

Everything from then on is history. Developing from that second encounter with her was a friendship that had to be God inspired. I became her personal chauffeur on all out of her out of town excursions. We traveled to so many different places together. Shopping, eating out, visiting, and going to the beauty shop, church programs, and many other places.

There was not a week that went by where we didn't spend at least one day together. We were together, during good times, and bad times, happy times and sad times. We learned to do as Dionne Warwick suggested in the song "That's what friends are For". We learned to keep smiling, keep shining because we knew we could count on each other. We had come to the realization that's what true friends are for; True friends, make sacrifices for each other. I've shared with her in the good times and vowed not to leave her as she goes through this rough time, because after all, "she's my friend"

My friend and her husband lived a quiet, peaceful life, with some socializing on occasions, but mostly a life of solitude. They enjoyed this type of existence and it carried on with my friend even after the passing of her husband. They were private people, not to the point they were recluses, but just private. Sometimes I would think that she was too cautious because she would shred any piece of paper that had her name on it. She would even tear the labels off the medicine bottles before throwing them away. Now with all the talk about identity theft, in reality, I can see that she was just being pro-active.

Knowing how secretive my friend was, one can only imagine how surprise I was when she asked me to take charge of her financial affairs. My immediate reply to her was an emphatic NO! The answer I gave her was not because I couldn't handle the task, because I had worked with finances on a previous job I held. Also I have an associate degree in banking/finance, but I told my friend that the reason why I didn't want to do it was because "I know how families are".

She didn't realize by asking me to do this, she was putting me in a very precarious position. Most people don't think highly of a person who interferes with family.

Again I said to her "I really don't want to do it." Her reply to me was "you are going to hurt my feelings" With that being said it was settled, I agreed to do it because I certainly did not want to do anything to hurt or disappoint her. Then the thought came to me, my friend is an adult, she in her right mind, with all her faculties and if this is what she wanted, why should I refuse her request based on what family would say. After seeing that there was no refusing her, I agreed. There was such an expression of relief that came across her face. She immediately contacted her attorney and the papers were drawn up.

Everything that happens in all of our lives can be traced back to an event in the bible. By me being put in charge of my friends finances reminded me of how Joseph was put in charge of all of Pharaoh's affairs. Again it was all in God's plan and God moves in a mysterious way.

On the day we went to the lawyer's office to sign and pick up the papers the secretary said to my friend, you have given her charge over everything. She can sell your house out from under you if she wants to. Her words did not offend me, she was just making sure my friend understood what she was doing. If people don't know you they automatically assume the worst. You have to prove yourself over and over again, and sometimes they come to believe in you and sometimes they don't. My friend abruptly said "she wouldn't do that" It was evident that she believed in me, she trusted me.

For several years after the papers were drawn up my friend still handled her own financial affairs. She was just being precautious in the event that if she ever needed someone they would already be in place. But now that I think about it, I am certain that she had definite insight that something was going to happen to alter life as she once knew it and she was right.

Those persons who live close to God, will be the first to say that He gives us warnings or a sense of things that are about to take place; this is the work of the Holy Spirit. When we don't take heed to the promptings of the Holy Spirit we get in trouble. The things that happened later on in my friend's life give credence to the fact that we must listen and obey when God speaks to us.

It was mid-day when the phone rang and after answering it I heard a weak almost inaudible voice say "I'm sick", It was my friend. I rushed up the hill to her house and found her seated on the bed, in pain and nauseated. Without hesitation I dialed 911 and she was transmitted to the local hospital. I phoned her nieces and nephews, and her step children to let them know what was going on. Several hours later she was transferred to another affiliate hospital. Various tests were performed but showed nothing.

My friend spent over a week in the hospital, and God allowed her to recover. We still to this day don't know what the problem was, but with the help of prayer, and antibiotics, she made it through.

The day before she was to be released from the hospital, one of her nurses said "I hear you are going to a nursing facility". Neither my friend nor I had made those types of arrangements, but I took it to mean that someone was working behind the scene without our knowledge. After hearing what the nurse said I told my friend you better get-up and get ready to get out of here because somebody is trying to put you in a nursing home. It is so hilarious now, but I have never seen an eighty one year old woman get into her pants so fast. She said we'll show them. And show them she did. My friend went home, and after a couple weeks of pampering from myself and our minister friend, she resumed doing everything that she was doing before that hospital stay. God had worked a miracle in her life, but hey, He's in the miracle working business.

Reflecting on that bout of sickness and her returning home, she opened up to me about a lot of things that had happened in her life, going back to her childhood. Something traumatic had happened to her, something that evidently her family didn't even know about. If they knew they never talked about it.

We both were seated in the kitchen and out of no where she told me she had been raped. This was something that I wasn't expecting to hear. She said it was by someone that she knew and he was her cousin. My friend told me that her father didn't even know it happened, because he would have killed the person.

My mind immediate went to 2nd Samuel chapter 13 which details Tamar's rape by her half-brother. It took two years, but Absalom got revenge on Ammon for what he had done to his sister.

After telling me about the rape, it was as if a load had been lifted off her shoulders. She didn't tell me this as if it were a secret, that I should keep confidential, but she told me this as if to say this is why I'm so private. The fact that she had been raped went a long way to explain why she had a hard time trusting people. It explained why she locked her doors, even in the day time, and kept her window curtains pulled shut all the time. When stopping to pump gas, she locked the doors of the car until I returned. It certainly explained her becoming tense whenever she had to deal with a male nurse.

Once you have experience something that traumatic, you never get over it. She had managed to get on with her life, but she never forgot it. As I listened to her telling me about the rape, never mentioning the person's name, I could see that even now it pained her. Not to the point of wanting to execute revenge like Absalom, but a pain of not allowing this to happen again.

Often we criticize people, classify them as strange without knowing their story. I think this is precisely why Jesus told us not to judge in Matthew 7:1. We never know what other people have experienced in life, which causes them to behave the way they do. Criticism comes easy when you don't know a person's story. There was some repenting that needed to take place, and I couldn't exclude myself. Often the thought, is it necessary to be this cautious came to my mind? After learning about the rape the answer to that question is yes, it is. There is always an uneasiness that leads one to believe if it happened once it can happen again.

My friend had told me that she had an hysterectomy early in life. I wondered if this stemmed from the rape. That explains why she never had children of her own.

More and more my friend talked a lot about the past. I didn't recognize it then but digressing back to earlier times in one's life could be the onset of dementia. Was this happening to my friend? No it couldn't be, so that thought was put out of my mind.

Pretty soon we were back to our old routine of hitting the malls, outlet stores, just enjoying each other's company. Life was good for my friend and wasn't too shabby for me either, because just being in her company and to see her happy made me happy. Glancing over and witnessing the smile that would come across her face from time to time, was enough to cheer me. Oh how I miss that smile.

That hospital stay proved to be only the beginning of many more to come in the life of my friend.

One summer evening I received a call to come to the hospital and when I got there I discovered that my friend had been in an automobile accident. It wasn't her fault, but she was utterly shaken, for nearly two years we went back and forward to the doctor and lawyer because of that accident. There were no broken bones, just bruises of both her body and mind. Not to mention her car was totaled. My friend no longer trusted her driving and judging from how she would be braking from the passenger side, she didn't trust mine. I guess that's what being in a car accident will do; it shatters a person nerves.

While she might not have trusted my driving, she trusted me with ever thing else and became more and more dependent upon me. The accident slowed her down considerably, and it was only the beginning of a downward spiral in her physical well-being.

There were several warning signs that something was going on in her body, but I guess she didn't want to accept it and I overlooked it. She was past her eighties and quite naturally I assumed that some of her ailments were due to her age. But soon it became apparent that what was going on with her was more than age related.

We had traveled to the outlet mall in Gaffney SC, and visited several shops, All of a sudden my friend became completely out of breath. We stopped walking and she sat down on one of the benches outside so she could rest. Her body was drained and by the time we got back to the car she was completely exhausted. This was something out of the ordinary, for she could usually draw circles around me when it came to shopping, but not this day. We returned home and nothing else was said about the incident.

Another sign that something was wrong was when we were out in the local community and she had a severe coughing attack, which caused her to have to struggle to get her breath. I pulled over in the parking lot of a convenience store and ran inside to get her something to drink. With tears streaming down her face, almost in a panic, she vowed never to smoke another cigarette. After a minute or two she got better. She knew off hand what the problem was. Her many years of cigarette smoking was beginning to take a toll on her.

As close as we were it was shocking to discover that my friend had been a heavy smoker. She had always managed to keep it from me. But in retrospect, that explains her sudden exit from the table whenever we were eating out; or her disappearing to the bath room at different intervals, she was going to grab a puff.

After that last episode of being breathless, I made her a doctor's appointment with her medical doctor, and she was referred to a specialist. It was confirmed she had COPD,(**Chronic obstructive pulmonary disease**). In her case it was caused by her many years of cigarette smoking. Not only was she a smoker, but her husband had been a smoker also. It was not only her smoking that had created this condition, but breathing second hand smoke also contributed to her lung disease.

The Pulmonary doctor explained that there was no cure, but the condition could be slowed down especially if she quit smoking. Thankfully she had already done that, but a lot of damage had already been done to her lungs.

With the news of her condition came oxygen therapy, nebulizers, and inhalers of all sorts. She had an inhaler for morning, one to use for emergencies, one to take both in the morning and evening, and pills to top them off. You pretty much had to be a pharmacist to keep up with her daily routine, and a banker to be able to afford all the COPD medications plus her other prescribed medicines.

After being diagnosed with COPD, coupled with still trying to get over the car accident, my friend slowed down even more. She stopped going shopping something she really enjoyed doing. She even stopped her visits to the beauty shop and going to church both of which were ritualistic to her. She was a very proud woman, and carrying oxygen around lowered her self-esteem. She became content with staying in the house and getting out only to go to the doctors; everything else, she knew she could count on me to do.

Her bank and pharmacist knew who I was because after the accident and with news of this new condition, it was I who handled the financial part of her life. To this day some of the bank tellers still refer to me by my friend's name, they realize afterward that this was just a slip of the tongue, but for years we were inseparable. Also her medical doctor and pulmonary doctor knew me because I was the one who made sure she made it to all her appointments on time. I can't count the many times we went to Greenville, Spartanburg, and Landrum keeping appointments.

When it came to grocery shopping even this was not a problem, because we had done it together for years; I knew her likes and dislikes. She was so particular about everything she bought. She didn't buy bananas that had spots on the bottom because she said the monkeys had been playing with them. Reach in the back to get the milk because it has the longer expiration date. Even pumping gas, she had a method for that also. She would say "pump it slow because you get more gas, if you pump it fast you get air." Even in paying her bills she had a routine. I knew the bills that had to be paid, and the time they had to be paid. She would say "if you pay the bills too early they think you have money". Wait and pay them a day or so before the due date. She had trained me well, but isn't that what mothers do?

My husband often commented that I was just like my friend. She had taught me to buy what was on sale, and if wasn't on sale wait until it goes on sale. She bought her summer clothes as the season was coming to an end and likewise her winter clothes. She explained that this was when the stores wanted to get rid of things so they mark them down to make room for the seasonal clothes that were coming in. "Great bargains are to be had" she would say. "If you don't need it now wait until it goes on sale". She wasn't a miser, but she did believe in saving whenever she could.

I remember once before she stopped going to the grocery store that she wanted a tomato and the price of tomatoes at the supermarket was more than she thought they should be so she said "I'll wait until they go on sale" I thought to my self, what kind of sense does this make? If you want a tomato you want it right now, not when it goes on sale. But that's how her mind worked.

Thinking about her spending habits and conservative ways, these two components are probably what enabled her to live comfortably all these years. Now I had become accustomed to her way of thinking when it came to shopping, and every time there was an item that interested me and the price I thought was too much, I would say "I'll wait until it goes on sale". Needless to say this irritated my husband. He would say what if it has sold, well "it wasn't for me" I would reply.

To show you how resourceful she was, one day I had to go to the bank and the teller noticed that my- to -do list was written on the back of an envelope that the bank mails to their customers giving their account information. I said my friend recycles everything. I also said to the teller "I could write a book about her." The teller laughed and said I'm sure you could Then she said "what kind of book would it be"? I said I can think of a million and one topics and each one would probably be a best-seller.

Now that I think about it, I could write a book from a number of genres pertaining to my friend. For instant, a cookbook could be compiled from all the recipes she shared with me over the years. My friend was an excellent cook and had worked in that capacity for a number of years for one or two prominent families in Tryon.

One family that she often talked about was the Mahler. I recent ran across an article about this family in the local newspaper and also found several photos of her serving dinner to the Mahler family. The exuberant smile on her face, proved she enjoyed what she was doing. Seeing the pictures she had of them and the newspaper article helped me put faces to this family she often talked about, she held them in high esteem.

My friend had numerous cookbooks of her own and in many of them she had made little notations where she added this and took that away, making the recipe her own. She had a recipe for almost everything: cakes, pies, lasagna, banana pudding, roast beef, turkey, and so much more. You name it she had a recipe for it.

Since she didn't believe in giving her cooking secrets away, I dare not betray her confidence by putting them in a book.

Another book I could write would be about investing. She always told me that she was the one who started her husband saving. A penny here and a penny there and pretty soon you have a dollar. She never looked at savings and investing in the short term, always the long term. She explained to me if you can put back ten dollars every week, in a year's time you would have saved five hundred and twenty dollars, not calculating accrued interest. Then she would say think about what that would add up to if you did it for ten years? She said you would have five thousand two hundred dollars not to mention the interest you would earn. Then she would say "that's how you get ahead". See that ten dollars as paying a bill that you owe. It is a bill you owe to yourself.

The Mahler family had a history with Kimberly Clark and each year at Christmas, they would give my friend so many shares of stock in that company. Over the years the stock increased in value and had numerous splits. Thank God for that stock, because it enabled her to live comfortably during her years of declining health. She did not have to worry about who would pay her nursing home bills, because she had saved for that time in her life.

At the time the Mahler family was giving her that stock, she really had no idea that it proved to be such a blessing to her.

But the book that I am writing is not about her cooking expertise, or her savings and investing techniques, but simply a book about what she is and was to me, my friend.

When the bank teller and I were joking about writing a book pertaining to my friend, I never thought that day would come so soon. Here I am reminiscing about my friend and putting all those memories down on paper. I wonder what she would say if she knew that her life is an open book now. The privacy that she had striven to maintain for years is now exposed to all who desires to read about it.

Putting the times we shared together down on paper will keep her alive to me. It's like when someone gives you a beautiful bouquet of flowers you want them to last forever so you take a picture of them. Long after the flowers have withered and died, you can go and look at the picture and you are reminded of their beauty all over again.

That explains why my friend took pictures of her azalea bushes, and other flowers when they were in full bloom. That explains why she would bring those pictures out and look at them. When fall had come and the blooms were gone, the pictures reminded her of the beauty they once held. When I read the pages of this book it will remind me of my friend.

The Flower Fades

God saw fit to pluck this lovely flower
and how it hurts your heart so,
to lose one that meant so much
and whose love to all did show.
You knew this day was coming
for it is the fate of all men,
yet each time it happens
the pain begins all over again.
May God comfort you at this time,
May He wipe your tears away
May His peace sustain and keep you
Is my prayer for you this day

Words written by Rev. Eleanor D. Miller

*The grass withers, the flower fades, But the
word of our God stands forever.*
Isaiah 40:8

Personal Reflections

Have you ever given any thought to what the "Great Gathering "will be like? I'm talking about the time when God calls all of us to stand before Him to be judged for the deeds done in this body, 2 Corinthians 5: 10. Will it be a time of joy and exuberance, or a time of sadness and despair. Your answer will be based on whether or not you will hear Him say, "well done my good and faithful servant, or depart from me you workers of iniquity I never knew you". If you haven't given that time much thought, take a few minutes to do so. Now write down your response.

_____

_____

_____

_____

_____

_____

_____

_____

_____

_____

_____

Now thank God for another chance to make the wrongs right, thank Him for His mercy.

Prayer

Dear God, teach us to cherish each moment we have with family and friends, for we know all too well that within a twinkling of an eye they can be taken away from us. Help us to look past any wrong they may have done to us, or any harsh words they may have uttered to us or about us. Help us to cling to the fond memories that we shared together. Help each of us remember that our lives are like the dandelions. With the slightest of breeze, we too can be scattered, never able to return to our original form again. Let your words abide in our hearts so that when that great gathering day comes, we will stand before you whole once again. In the name of Jesus the Christ I pray.

Amen

4

Preparing For The End

My friend never waited to the last minute to do anything, she believed in being ahead of the game, but she gave me an eerie feeling when one day out of the blue she started talking about her funeral. As I stated earlier, I believe God gives us insight into some of the things which are about to transpire in our lives, so he evidently had made her aware that her time was drawing near.

She had several visits from one mortician and she liked his demeanor and so she had decided early on that she wanted him to handle her final arrangements. She even knew where her funeral would take place, her church of course, and even who would participate down to the persons giving remarks. My friend did not want to be a burden to anyone, and so she handled this matter herself, I just followed her wishes by putting them all down on paper.

This gives credence to what kind of person she was, even in death, she was thinking about others. Although I felt like pre-planning her funeral was a little premature, it became apparent later on that she knew exactly what she was doing.

Another incident which cause the physical health of my friend to deteriorate even more happened one night before retiring to bed in early December 2011.

The phone rang and the person on the other end, asked me to go check on my friend; she had fallen and couldn't get up. Immediately I rushed to get to her. After getting to the house, I was unable to get in because she had locked the storm door before going to bed. I had a key to the inside door but not the storm door. Somehow she was able to make it to the door and open it. I helped her back to her bedroom, checked to make sure she was okay, tucked her in and left. That next morning she phoned me again and said "I think my leg is broken." I immediately went to her aide and found her seated on her bed. She had broken out in a cold sweat therefore I knew something was definitely wrong. I managed to get her dressed and the ambulance took her to the hospital. She was right; her hip had been broken as a result of the fall. She proceeded to explain what had happen to cause her to fall. "I was reaching for the telephone beside the bed, and fell out" she said. Her bed was practically on the floor, but as a person ages, a simple fall can do so much damage. A hip replacement was done and with several weeks of therapy and after spending six more weeks in rehabilitation at a the local nursing facility she was able to walk again using a walker.

This time after returning home from the broken hip, there was a noticeable change in my friend. She began calling her family and asking them if she had anything in her house that they wanted. She wanted them to get it before she passed so that there would be no disagreements.

Although I did not grasp it at the time, she was making preparations to die. She had come to the conclusion that material things no longer mattered anymore.

It was at that time that she had me to make a list of everything in her house. I did so, just as she had asked, listing things room by room. As I went over the list with her, she would have me to write down a name by a certain item. She would say so and so wanted this or so and so wanted that.

Some of the ones she asked if they wanted anything of hers gave no reply, because they didn't feel it was right, but they failed to understand this is what she wanted. She wanted her family to have something to remember her by.

She would always say to me if there is anything in here you want, get it. And my reply to her would be I can't take your things. "You're not taking it I'm giving it to you" she would say. But I couldn't bring myself to take anything. Doing so to me would mean accepting that the end was near and that was something that I wasn't prepared to do at this time; Perhaps that is how her family members felt also.

As I stare at her, I'm just expecting her to turn over and say to me "can you help me out of this bed?" She has pulled through on so many other occasions. Her will power has been more than some people half her age. This year prior to this bout of sickness, she has been in the hospital on three or four other occasions, always bouncing back and continuing to move on. But this time it seems like her resilience is at an all-time low.

My nights were spent wondering if I would get a call alerting me to something going on with my friend. My friend had signed up for the medical call service, and it proved to be an invaluable service, because that dreaded call that I had anticipated for so long came.

It was early morning, about 5a.m. when the phone rang. I answered and it was the medical call service on the other end. They told me my friend had fallen in the bathroom, and couldn't get up. As I scrambled to get dress I was terrified and wasted no time getting to her. She had hit her head on the bath tub. The ambulance was summoned and she was transported to the hospital. X-rays and a MRI was done which showed nothing. After lying in the emergency room from 5a.m. in the morning to 5p.m. that evening she was released to return home. The ER doctor concluded that perhaps she had been weakened from a lack of oxygen. I thought to release her was a mistake, but signed her out anyway.

She had only been back home for thirty minutes or less, when she fell again. This time she had fallen face down with the medical call button under her, therefore she could not call for help. I had just run downhill to retrieve some items; thankfully I wasn't gone long. If I had not returned as soon as I did things could have been much worse than they were

Once again the ambulance was summoned. The paramedics checked her out and she was not transmitted at that time. About 2:30 in the morning I received a call from the lady staying the night, saying that my friend was in pain. Again I rushed to her side and ended up back at the emergency room. Later she was admitted to the hospital for observations.

Although the CT scan and the MRI didn't show anything, there was definitely something going on with my friend. She was so confused, her speech was slurred, even sounding muffled at times. After several days she was released but needing 24 hour care; she slowly went downhill from there. Each fall she experienced only made her that much weaker, never recovering fully from them.

For two weeks we provided round the clock care at home. I would stay with her from six o'clock in the morning until four o'clock that evening. Another girl would come from four to ten and another lady from ten to six. This worked for a couple of weeks, but it became evident that her care required so much more than we could give her at home. Something else had to be done.

How do I approach the subject of asking my friend to leave her home? The place that holds the memories of the time shared with her husband. But again God moves in mysterious ways...

It is less than a month before Christmas and two of her great nieces paid her a visit. They had heard about the fall and suggested to her that she go to a home where she could be watched around the clock. She always thought that day would never come. You can imagine how sad she was when that subject was brought up, but she knew as well as I that it was time. Her words that day to her great nieces were "who would have ever thought?" I knew what she meant, who would have ever thought that I would end up in a nursing home? Many persons who are in their good health never imagine the time will come when they will be dependent on someone else to take care of them. But the word often speaks of it. In John chapter 21 verse 18 reads "Verily, verily I say unto thee, when thou wast young, thou girdedst thyself and walkedst whither thou wouldest; but when thou shalt be old, thou shalt stretch forth thy hands, and another shall gird thee, and carry thee whither thou wouldest not. (KJV)

Her mind became flood with many thoughts and she began to ask so many questions, "where will I go, who will live in my house, when am I going to my new home?" She knew that if she left her home, she wouldn't be coming back; life as she once knew it was gone. But in spite of all the changes coming her way, I hope she knew that I would still be there for her no matter where she went and she could count on me. After all we were true friends, our friendship would last forever.

Several days before my friend's going to the nursing facility, reality hit me like a ton of bricks. I cried, and cried, and cried. It felt almost like the sorrow I felt after receiving word that mother had passed.

There was something unusual about the day before mother had passed. I got up from bed, fixed breakfast and retired to the living room to study the bible. As I sat on the couch, reading and taking time for meditation a small voice spoke to me and said "go see your mother" The voice even told me what to say to her. Tell her to take her rest and reassure her that you will look after your brothers and sisters. Knowing that this was the voice of the Lord speaking to me, I got dressed and went straight to the hospital.

I told mother just what I had been instructed to say. And she let out a big sigh. This was what she was waiting to hear. Later that night mother passed.

It was a nice quiet night and I had already retired to bed when I got the phone call. The nurse on the other end said "Your mother has passed." I got dressed and went to the hospital. Mother was still in her room. She looked so pretty and peaceful lying in bed and I knew she was at rest. My heart was broken, but I knew that God in time would mend it. He had everything under control. What I needed to do was to trust Him and rely on Him.

Broken

You feel so empty now
because someone so dear is gone,
your heart has been broken
and you feel so all alone.
But in the midst of your sorrow,
in the midst of your pain,
know that the hurt won't last forever
you will laugh again.
God will take you in His loving hands
and mend your brokenness;
remold you and reshape you
He'll do what He does best.
He will never leave you nor forsake you,
He'll be with you all the way;
that's because He is the potter
and we are all His clay.

Words written by: Reverend Eleanor D. Miller

And the vessel that he made of clay was marred in the hand of the potter, so he made it again another vessel, as seemed good to the potter to make it.

Jeremiah 18:4

Prayer

*Dear Lord, thank you for being a God of a second chance.
In all truths, you are a God of many chances. For when our
lives are marred because of wrong words, actions, and deeds,
you allow us to see our mistakes and give us an opportunity to
repent of them. Not only do you take away the hurt but you
remove the scars of our brokenness. Only you are able to make
the rough edges smooth. Thank you for your reshaping power.*

Amen

Personal Reflections

Are there areas in your life that you need God to reshape? Genesis 1:27 says that You created man in Your image, in the image of God created he him; male and female created he them. Do you bear the image of God? Knowing that God is love, does your life exemplify love? Write down the ways that you bear the image of God in your words, actions and deeds.

_____

_____

_____

_____

_____

_____

_____

_____

_____

_____

_____

If you realize something is lacking, pray that God reshape you and mold you into what He would have you to be.

I often wonder what my life would have been like if my friend hadn't become a part of it. Would I have fallen in a state of depression because of the loss of my mother and remained there. Did God know that I needed someone to help me beyond this most grievous loss? Of course he did after all he knows everything. The words of Solomon in the book of Ecclesiastes chapter 3 reads to everything there is a season… so He worked it out that when mother's season to die had come, God who is Omniscient, had someone who could help me through it, my friend.

But now I wonder who will help me get through the loss of my friend?

In order to have a friend you must first show yourself friendly. But there is a friend who sticks closer that a brother Proverbs 18:24. That friend is Jesus. So I rely on him to get me through, because he knows.

God Knows our Season

A leaf has fallen from your family tree,
and oh how your heart must ache;
But find consolation in knowing that
God never makes a mistake.
He has caught that fallen leaf with His heavenly rake.
God has gathered your loved-one
and taken them to a place of eternal rest
and while you might not understand it now,
remember that God knows best.
Our season too is coming,
whether winter, spring, summer or fall
to meet our maker, the one who created all.
We share in your sorrow now, we pray for you too,
and we leave the rest to God to do what he knows
how to do. He will lead you and direct you,
He will carry you through,
He will finish where we leave off, after
doing all that we can do.

Words by: Reverend Eleanor D. Miller

To everything there is a season, a time for every purpose under the heaven: A time to be born and a time to die; A time to plant, And a time to pluck what is planted;

Ecclesiastes 3:1,2

Prayer

Dear God with an humbled and thankful heart I say thank you for knowing everything. I'm glad that everything happens according to your time table not mine. You know when to come and you know how to come. Help me to trust your timing.

Amen

Personal Reflections

Are there some things that you are waiting on God to do in your life? If so write them down.

_____

_____

_____

_____

_____

_____

_____

_____

_____

_____

Do you have the faith and the confidence in God to bring those things to pass? Are you willing to wait?

Isaiah 40:31:*They that wait upon the Lord shall renew their strength, they shall mount up on wings as eagles, they shall run and not get weary, they shall run and not faint.*

My friend has been in the rehab part of the local nursing home for a month now, and at times it seemed like she was making progress, but maybe that was just wishful thinking on my part. One day she would be her old self, alert and full or energy, the next day it would be a totally different story, she would be completely out of it.

Today was one of those good days I mentioned. My friend was just like her old self. Talking, laughing, and just enjoying family and friends. Her therapy was going quite well too. She had been known to get in one of her moods and refuse therapy, but according to the therapist this day she was on point.

My heart was overjoyed just to see her happy and content. She was eating and that is always a good sign of improvement. Could this mean that she was on the road to recover? Did it mean that one more time she has dodged the bullet and soon she would be back at home? Oh how I had prayed that this was the case, but sadly my enthusiasm was short lived.

Since the nursing facility was only about two miles from my home, I would visit her twice a day; arriving early in the morning and staying until after lunch and returning around five in the evening and staying long enough to tuck her in for the night.

Recalling one of my evening visits with her she began rambling. She envisioned herself as being in the country. She had grew up in the country, so I assumed that she was just remembering a time in her childhood? Perhaps her mind was going back to sweeter, happier times in her life. When we are small children, we are so carefree. We don't have to worry about this or that, because everything is taken care of for us. I know that there have been times that my mind would regress back to my childhood memories; a time when I did not have a worry in the world.

From her comments, she found peace and solitude being in the country, even mentioning the sound of rain. I remember saying to her, "the country is so pretty, quiet and peaceful and the rain has a way of washing the earth and making it clean. Although her comments were strange, everything she said I just went along with her always trying to reassure her that no matter where she was, country or city, she was going to be alright, because God was with her. The scripture used to confirm this was Matthew 28:20 *lo I am with you always, even unto the end of the age.* She enjoyed hearing scripture and prayer.

Christmas has come and gone and God had allowed my friend to be with us a little while longer. So many of her family and friends visited during the holidays not knowing if this would be the last Christmas they would share with her. She even had a surprise visit from her two step children.

It was good that they had come because a decision had to be made about where my friend would go after rehab. Going home was definitely not an option at this time because she still needed twenty four hour care. Knowing this, we looked into assisted living at the facility where she was now. After discussing the matter with my friend and others, it was agreed that this is where she would stay.

The transition to her new room was good, because many of those responsible for her care in rehab would also assist in her care in the new wing of the facility where she would be. It was only a matter of walking down the hall, but it was hard to get her to understand that. There was one or two times she asked why she had to leave the room where she was. I would say someone else needs this room more than you.

Because of her lack of understanding and remembering, it was apparent that dementia had set in. That explained many of the comments that she would make from time to time. Dementia was just another condition added to the list of other things that were going on with her.

But even with all her illnesses, for several weeks she continued to improve. She had settled into her new room and seemed to be enjoying her home away from home. But then she began to have the spikes in blood pressure again. This coupled with difficulty breathing because of the COPD and the frequent anxiety attacks she had been experiencing, let us know that her condition was worsening and was beginning to take a toll on her. Over and over I tried to reassure myself that she would get beyond this difficult time, after all, when she came to the facility several months earlier, everyone thought that her life would soon be over. We had become accustomed to the fluctuations with her condition-the ups and downs. Although she had come out of rehab the uncertainty continued.

There would be times when she would be so confused, hallucinating, rapid breathing and escalated blood pressure until she required being given something to lower her blood pressure and calm her down. This medication would always zap her and leave her with no strength to even sit up. Sometimes she wouldn't even know that I had been in the room. I hated to see her like this and disliked her being given that medication, but I knew that it was necessary.

And as if what she was suffering through now wasn't enough, depression set in, which caused her to just stay in bed the majority of time, sleeping. The lack of activity, wasn't good because one of the keys to living longer for persons with COPD is exercise. But my friend had gotten to the point where she had very little energy to do anything, talking was even a struggle.

Still I would read to her from the prayer book that sits on her night stand, hoping that she would hear something to bring her back to the vibrant person she use to be, but it never happened. She had come to that point where she was ready to go home. On several occasions she mentioned going home to others, and they automatically assumed she meant back to her house. But she was not talking about her earthly home, but her heavenly home. She knew the scriptures especially the scripture that says Jesus was going away to prepare a place for us, that where he is we can be also. John 14:3. She had come to the time in her life where she was ready to go meet Jesus.

But while she was ready to go, I still was not ready to let her go. In retrospect I can see now how selfish this was. How could I insist that she fight to live when she wanted to go? At the time I was trying to hold on to my friend as long as possible. Therefore when she didn't want to eat I would insist "you have to eat something, to keep up your strength", and when she didn't want to drink, I would say you have to keep hydrated. How could I sit idle and watch her starve herself to death? I couldn't and so each day from the time she was moved to assisted living, my routine would include eating lunch with my friend. Sometimes she would only take a bite or two, and take one or two sips from a glass of tea, but that was better than nothing.

The nurses and CNAs would often tell me that she perks up when you are present, you can get her going. That stemmed from the fact that for the last ten or eleven years we were always together and had developed a special bond. When the workers didn't understand her comments at times because of her inability to form correct sentences, I would tell them what she meant.

Then came the time when my presence wouldn't motivate her to eat. How sad it was to witness her slowly fading away.

Trying to prepare myself for what seemed to be the inevitable; I began to read about end-of-life issues and the signs and symptoms of impending death. Sometimes guilt would overwhelm me because it seemed as though I was giving up on her, but I wasn't. I just couldn't stand the thoughts of my friend leaving and I not be able to say goodbye, therefore I wanted to be able to discern when time was near so I could be there.

There was a wealth of information available pertaining to what to expect when there is only months, weeks, days, or hours left for a person to live.

There were directives regarding what to do after death occurs. But what caught my attention were the comments that often times people hang-on waiting to get permission from a loved one to go. Whose permission was my friend waiting on?

My friend had mentioned going home to others on several occasions, but never once did she say anything of that nature to me until one morning days prior to her demise.

It was early morning and the phone rang, I recognized the number and my heart rhythm sped up, it was the nursing facility. The person on the other end said that my friend had fallen. She's okay, but we just wanted you to be aware of it.

Hurriedly I got dressed and made my way to her. Standing beside her bedside she said these words "I'm going" and let out one of the biggest laughs. The only thing that I could think to say to her was its okay to go, you will be alright. There was no doubt in my mind that she knew she was getting ready to go home.

Inadvertently I had given her my permission to go. I knew it had to be God speaking through me in order for me to utter those words to her. The same way God had sent someone to suggest that it was time for her to go to a nursing facility, He took over and guided the words "it's alright to go" out of my mouth, giving her permission to go to be with God.

The agony and pain she had suffered through for weeks had left her face thin and her skin color gray and dull. All these were signs that she was beginning to make the transition, and if all she needed was me to say it's alright, how could I withhold that from her, no matter how bad I wanted her to stay.

She had definitely suffered enough. God knew that I could never speak those words, He through the Holy Spirit helped me to do what I could not and did not want to do. Even though I had given her my permission to go, she still hung on to life for months after that.

With the dementia progressing rapidly, she had become at times combative. She would lash out at the ones providing care for her, and refused to do the thing they bid her to do, such as getting dressed and undressed. She wouldn't want to live with such a negative disposition, this was not her nature and it certainly wasn't how she would want to be remembered.

On one particular occasion I had sat all day with her and witnessed her drift in and out of consciousness, moaning and groaning, coughing and just before night fall I couldn't watch her suffer any longer so I insisted she be sent to the hospital.

After being looked at in the emergency room and having chest X-rays taken it was confirmed she had pneumonia. She wasn't admitted to the hospital but was sent back to the nursing facility with prescribed antibiotics.

Deep with in my spirit I knew why she hadn't been admitted, because ultimately, there was nothing else to be done. Just like she had told me she was going, she knew. And even though I didn't want to accept it, I knew also. But I also realized that time was in God's hands. She wasn't going anywhere until he got ready for her to go. But still there were some unanswered questions that lingered in my mind and there was no longer putting off the question of how much time my friend had left, so I asked the doctor. She was as candid as she could be, speaking cautiously to see what my perception of the matter was.

She confirmed that with all that was going on with my friend and the medical conditions she had, that death was inevitable, but she could not say when.

"When would be an appropriate time to fill her family in" I asked looking intently at her with tear filled eyes. Of course she left that up to me.

I dared not rob her family members of spending precious time with my friend, so the news was given to them immediately. Now all we could do was just wait and see, and accept whatever God had in store for my friend.

We had been through this so many times in the past. I remember just a couple of months earlier when I began this book, I had kept bedside visual because it was thought she wouldn't last another week, and then she made a dramatic turn around. But somehow this time things seemed totally different.

Waiting, watching, praying, singing, and reading, I am reminded about a woman in the bible who is referred to as a disciple (Acts 9:36-42) her name was Dorcas /Tabitha. According to the bible Dorcas was a woman who was full of good works.

She was a woman who sewed and made garments for persons in need, using her own resources to make sure others were taken care of.

This sounded so much like my friend. She was constantly giving of herself and her resources to help others. No one really knew the extent of her giving beside me, and the ones who were the recipient of her generosity. One day Dorcas died and the people of the area were terribly devastated at her death. In the bible Apostle Peter was in a nearby town so the people sent for him to come. Without hesitation Peter went to where they had laid Dorcas making preparation for her burial, and after praying Dorcas was miraculous raised to life again. What a miracle and I can almost hear the shouts of acclamation to have her presented alive to the people.

Once the breath has left my friend's body, I knew that she will not be raised to a physical body, but she shall be raised to a new spiritual body. She will not get that body as a result of her good works, but because of her faith in God. She knew better than anyone else that faith without works is dead. She had faith and she showed it by her works (acts of love) to others the same as Dorcas.

Watching day after day as my friend grew weaker, I read even more books and articles pertaining to end-of-life symptoms, and included grief management in my reading. There was so much information to grasp. No one really knows how they will respond until death happens, but I just didn't want to be caught off guard. But in all of my reading there was one aspect of death that I never read anything about. I had read nothing that would prepare me for what I call the *"other side of grief, greed."* It was shocking to say the least, to see how this aspect of death reared its ugly head at the last stage of my friend's illness. Is this what my friend would have wanted? I could definitely say the answer to that question is an emphatic no.

After telling the family of the doctor's prognosis concerning my friend, I was expecting everyone to be as saddened as I was; my heart was breaking. But judging from the actions of some, not all of her family members, it was a matter of when is she going to expire, and what's in it for me? I'm sure they all were saddened to hear of her prognosis, but some had a funny way of showing it.

In not so many words, some family members implied that my services were no longer needed, as if to say we will take over now. Some people can be so cruel.

Was it that they thought I was getting paid? I took their comments and innuendoes in stride and remained vigilant by my friend's bedside. After all what price can you put on true friendship? True friendship is endless, it is priceless.

After such vivid display of greed, I felt it time to deal with the last aspect of my friend's life, her funeral. If she leaves this world broke, it will be alright at least her exit will be the way she wanted it.

As I mentioned earlier, my friend had entrusted her final arrangements to me. Although I had put her wishes down on paper, I had put off making them as long as I could. Now was the time to make that dreaded trip to the mortuary. With the folder in hand detailing her last wishes I arrived at the funeral home and was greeted by the Director of funeral services. He was so courteous and made such a grievance task less painful.

I gave him my friend's name and explained that she desired this to be done so there would not be a burden on her family. She was always thinking ahead, in life and even in death. Some might have thought this was selfish, but it wasn't. My friend couldn't stand the thought of imposing on anyone. If she could do things herself, she would.

Step by step we went through every aspect of her final arrangement and burial. I got the total cost and several days later I paid the mortician. Now when the time comes, whether days, weeks, months or years from now, everything will be as she wanted it down to the outline of the service.

It wasn't hard outlining how the service would be carried out because we were both Methodist. She was African Methodist and I Christian Methodist, in both churches, the order of service is pretty much the same. She already had her cemetery plot picked out and paid for: she was to rest between her father and late husband.

To have this task completed was such a relief, and to do it like she wanted was an even greater relief. I must confess I did omit one thing that she wanted, and that was for me to make remarks. My reasons for not including myself are personal, and there is no need to write about them. As I exited the mortuary, I thought to myself, my friend will be put away in style. She deserved no less because she was a stylish lady. Just one peek in her closet will give credence to the fact that she loved to dress and knew how to dress. Dresses, suits, handbags and shoes galore fill her closets. Although she loved nice things, she didn't treasure them. I know of several occasions when she would invite persons over and just give them bags of her finest attire, she was just that kind of person. My friend knew it was better to give than receive, my she taught me so much.

The following months seemed to have been the hardest that my friend had endured since being in the nursing facility. She was now on the skilled nursing unit. Even more so than ever I made sure that I was there every day. It was so hard because many of the residents on this hall could hardly do anything for themselves. Watching them let me know that a lot of extra care and attention was needed. Some couldn't talk, get up on their own or even bath themselves. Moving to this unit let me know that unless a miracle happened, this would be the same predicament my friend would be in. How I needed strength to help me continue to be by her side. I knew that I couldn't abandoned her now, after all we were friends.

Prayer

Dear God thank you for your strength that strengthens me. For your word says When we are *weak* in ourselves, then we are *strong* in the grace of our Lord. It is your grace that sustains us in our weakest hour. Continue to strengthen me for what ever lies ahead. And keep reminding me that I can do all things through Christ... In the name of Jesus, I pray

Amen.

Personal Reflections

What task has God helped you to perform lately?

_____

_____

_____

_____

_____

_____

_____

_____

_____

_____

Philippian 4:13 *I can do all things through Christ which strengthens me.*

Today a long time acquaintance of my friend was brought into the facility for rehabilitation. They had known each other for years, and when her eyes first met his, I couldn't help but notice the expression of excitement and gladness that she exhibited.

They had their meals in the same dining hall before she was placed in the skilled unit. On one occasion when my friend was leaving the dining hall he caught her hand and said to her, "I'll see you later, or I'll see you when we get to the other side." He was speaking of getting to heaven. It was apparent that he knew his time on this side wasn't long. My friend smiled at him but said nothing.

I received word that he passed this week. He made it to the other side before my friend. Now I must find the appropriate time and the best way to break the news to my friend that he is gone. Again I am reminded of the fact that God will not put more on us than we can bear and I know that when the right time comes to tell her, he will give me words to say to her. How ironic, a friend telling a friend that a friend has passed on.

The Saturday before his funeral on Monday I broke the news to my friend that he had passed. She was saddened to hear the news, but had so many questions about him. How old was he, how many children did he have, was he the oldest of his siblings, thing she already knew but was unable to bring to her mind because of the physical state that she was in. I answered all her questions with what I knew about him, but if I had made it up she won't have known the difference, because within minutes of me telling her, what I said had eluded her memory. Maybe this was a good thing, for the news of his passing was soon gone also.

In a day or so we will be celebrating Easter 2014. How I wished that my friend could attend Easter sunrise service. She enjoyed participating in her church activities before she became ill. Cooking and baking for various church functions was something she loved to do. However, visiting her the Saturday before Easter let me know that going to church was definitely out of the question, because this was one of her bad days.

The whole time I was with her she was hallucinating and talking out of her head. Maybe it was a reaction to some of her medication, but she totally was out of it. The blank stares, the talking to family member that weren't present and remembering things as far back as her childhood were just a few of the things that she was doing. My visit lasted for almost two hours, and she never got better. Perhaps a good night sleep will calm her down and she will be back to herself somewhat.

This is what I thought and so I left. Just before approaching the exit door I wondered was this the beginning of the end? Should I stay because of all the things that I had read about the end of life process? All the symptoms were there, but she had done this the whole time she had been in the nursing facility. I perceived this as being another false alarm, and therefore continued to leave.

The next day would be Easter Sunday, and my family probably would be expecting a big dinner. There is an old saying that goes "like mother, like daughter" and when it came to cooking family dinners during the holidays I had picked up on that ritual from mom.

My family had not come to grasp with the fact that true friendship requires sacrifices. While I was ready to give up a Sunday dinner for a friend they weren't. Understanding comes with time, Perhaps one day they will get the meaning of true friendship and what it entails. But until that time, I continued with the usual preparation for Easter dinner.

As I thought about true friendship, I was reminded of King David in the bible. He found out that he had a true friend. That friend's name was Jonathan, the son of King Saul, David's enemy. After Saul had lost favor in God's eyes because of disobedience, David, the little shepherd boy was anointed the next king over Israel by Samuel.

Because David was a skilled musician, he found himself in Saul's home playing his harp for him. Only David's music could subside the evil spirit that would sometimes come over Saul. Eventually David ended up staying in Saul home and after realizing that his kingship would eventually come to an in, and David would be the next king, Saul came to despise David and on several occasions he tried to kill him.

But David found a friend in Jonathan. Jonathan went against his father Saul, and saved David's life. In 1st Samuel chapter 18verse 1 the scripture says, And it came to pass, when he had made an end of speaking unto Saul, that the soul of Jonathan was knit with the soul of David, and Jonathan loved him as his own soul.

In Matthew Henry's concise Commentary he writes this pertaining to 1st Samuel chapter 18:1-5 "The friendship of David and Jonathan was the effect of Divine grace, which produces in true believers one heart and one soul, and causes them to love each other. This union of souls is from partaking in the Spirit of Christ. Where God unites hearts, carnal matters are too weak to separate them."

To some extent this defines my friend's and I relationship. It came about as a result of Divine grace.

The hymnist wrote through many dangers, toils and snares I have already come; Tis Grace that brought me safe thus far and Grace will lead me home. *John Newton (1725-1807)*. What a profound acknowledgement of the awesome love that God has for His creation: that in the most disturbing circumstances, God's Grace is with us, leading and directing us.

God's Amazing Grace had brought my friend through many, many, trials and tribulations. It was God's Grace that had raised her up off her sick bed on numerous occasions. She definitely knew where her help came from. And it will be God's Amazing grace that will draw my friend unto Himself when her time to depart from this side comes.

Prayer

*Dear God thank you for your Amazing Grace
In the times when I feel so alone and heartbroken,
Your Amazing Grace gives me the assurance that you are
always by my side. You soothe all my heart pains and you
take away all of my fears about what tomorrow holds. The
future is in your hands. Therefore I lean and depend on your
sustaining power which keeps me going day after day. In
the times when I feel like giving up, I can go on because of
your Amazing Grace that saved me. And I know that you
saved me not just for me, but for someone else
also. You saved me so that I could be here for
my friend, Dear God you are Amazing.
Thank you for your Amazing Grace.*

Personal Reflections

Can you recall a time when you knew beyond a shadow of a doubt that it was God's Amazing Grace that sustained you? Take a minute to explain.

_____

_____

_____

_____

_____

_____

_____

_____

_____

_____

Grace: The free, unmerited favor of God; as manifested in the salvation of sinner and the bestowal of blessings.

How ironic it is that I began this book reflecting on a hymn written by a poet named William Cowper, and now as I draw near to the end of the book, I'm reflecting on a hymn written by another hymnist or poet, John Newton. John Newton penned the words to Amazing Grace and the irony is both of these men although different in so many ways, had so much in common. Both had lost their mothers at an early age, both were preachers, and both were poets or hymnist. Another irony is the two ended up being friends, and remained friends even after Newton moved away from Olney where he and Cowper resided. But before they separated, they collaborated together and compiled a hymnal. Many of the hymns that are included in that hymnal are favorites of a lot of people today, church goers or not.

At a low point in Cowper's life he found someone who he was able to relate to; someone who cared enough for him to want to help him through the darkest times in his life. There was only so much that Newton was able to do to help Cowper, but he was there to do what he could.

Reading about these two friends life story motivates me even more to be by the side of my friend. I know that there is only so much that I can do, but at least she knows that she is not alone.

Jesus reminded his disciples that ...lo I am with you always *(Matthew 28:20)*. The reassurance that no matter what obstacles and dilemma the disciples found themselves in, Jesus promised he would be there working behind the scenes to bring about an expected end. He is still working things out in life and even in death. God works through people. He has someone in place to work behind the scene to make sure His plans are carried out. Although we may not understand all His ways we know that His word is true.

The scripture tells us, *and we know that all things work together for good to them that love God, to them who are the called according to his purpose.* **Romans 8:28 KJV**

Prayer

Dear God because you are always with us, I know that
you are the one who helps us over come our fears, and
gives us the ability to persevere to do the work that you
have assigned us to do. Sometimes we are weakened
and saddened when we have to face suffering, among
family and friends, but knowing that even in the midst
of suffering you are there, reassuring us and helping us
do the things that must be done. Your word tells us to
deny ourselves and take up our cross and follow you. It
is at these times that we deny the heart pains that we
are feeling and try even harder to alleviate the pain of
others. When I think that I can't go on you help me
go a little bit further. Although I'm sad, I'm hurting, I
wipe the tears from my eyes, put a smile on my face and
push open the door to where the sick is lying and say
Good Morning!

Personal Reflections

Has there ever been a time when you had to put aside your true feelings in order to help someone else deal with a problem or dilemma they were facing? If so write it down.

_____

_____

_____

_____

_____

_____

_____

_____

_____

_____

As you reflect on that time, know that God will send someone your way to help you deal with what you are experiencing right now.

It is a good morning today, for my friend seems so much like her old self. How excited I was to see her sitting in her wheel chair alert and so responsive to the things going on around her. During my visit today we talked about so many things and reminisced about the past.

My friend asked me when I had been to Tanners; this was one of our favorite shopping spots. I told her I hadn't been since the two of us were there. She smiled and said we use to go everywhere. We sure did and I miss that I replied. We even talked about some of our favorite eating places and we discussed some of the ones that weren't so good, some of them were quite unpleasant to say the least.

My how I enjoyed today's visit, which lasted hours. I left feeling good about our time together and wished that all of my visits with her could be like this one. It was like the sun breaking through the clouds after a hard rain. How my soul was refreshed for what I had experience with my friend this day.

As the sun slowly peeks through the sky that was once
darkened by the storm, is the same way that the Son
will bring light into the life that has been darkened by
sorrow and grieve. At that moment when the storm
is raging one feels as though the storm will rage
on forever, then out of nowhere the sky clears
up; the lightning and thundering cease and
suddenly it is at that moment you realize that
the storm has passed. But until the winds of grieve
and sorrow subside, and the tears like rain stop
flowing, it is good to know that God will shelter us.

Psalms 91:1
He who dwells in the shelter of the Most High
Will abide in the shadow of the Almighty.

Personal Reflections

Has God ever sheltered you and protected you from danger? As you recall those times, be reminded that if He did it once He will do it again. The storms will cease, the sun will shine.

_____

_____

_____

_____

_____

_____

_____

_____

_____

_____

Isn't it good to know that behind every rainy and cloudy day, the sun will shine?

Prayer

Dear God I pray that you will continue to shelter me from this storm that I am going through. Shield me, protect me, and keep me safe in you loving arms, so that I may make it through in peace: peace of heart, peace of soul and peace of mind. Peace in knowing that your love covers me. And dear God, I pray that you will continue to let my friend abide in your shadow, bearing your image as she goes through this difficult time in life. You have said that I will never leave you nor forsake you, I will be with you always, even to the end…As you were there in the beginning, speaking light in existence, I know that you will be there in the end rolling the storm clouds away in order that light can shine forth into the darkness that death imparts. I pray in the name of your darling Son, Jesus, the Christ, my Savior.

Amen

June 24, 2014

Happy Birthday to you, are the words that I greeted my friend with this morning. She had made it to her eighty seventh birthday and with all that she had been through this past year, this birthday was really something to celebrate. I know that it was only by the grace of God that she was spared to see this day. I was so happy for her.

All the nursing facility nurses and administrative staff joined together and sang happy birthday to my friend. She was so overjoyed. This really made her day. When asked how old are you? She replied seventy five. I don't know if she said that As a joke or if she thought she was seventy five I dared not correct her. She had passed seventy five years of age twelve years ago. At that age, seventy five, she was as active as any fifty year old. The old saying goes; you are as young as you feel, so if she felt like she was seventy five today, then I was glad to go along with her.

This was going to be a long day for her, and I knew that throughout the day other relatives would be dropping by; therefore I made my visit short. I wished her happy birthday again and left.

As I sit here today thinking about all the people in the nursing facility that have transitioned, I can't help but feel saddened. Since June of last year a total of ten persons if not more, have gone on, the latest being my friend's roommate. Her roommate was a dear sweet person, and my friend had taken a liking to her.

A week earlier her roommate had been sent out to the hospital and from the time her roommate returned back to the nursing facility my friend took it upon herself to be her personal companion. She had become so attached to her until she didn't want to leave the room to go eat, because she didn't want to leave her roommate all alone. My friend's roommate slow decline lasted for about two weeks, and during that time I would sing songs to her and pray with her. She never spoke, but her eyes told me that she was aware of what was going on. My friend was so pleased that I took time from my visit with her to minister to her roommate.

Then early one morning her roommate took her last breath. When I went to visit my friend later that same morning she told me she was gone. I could see she was shaken, but her conscious was clear, because even in her condition, she had done all she could for her. My only regret is that I never took a picture of the two of them together. Her roommate is gone, but she will never be forgotten, at least not by my friend.

As I sit here today, thinking back to the time my friend first came to the nursing facility, I realize it has been two years now. No one would have ever believed that my friend would be here today, but she is. Her breathing is getting worse, and from all the pamphlets I have read, it will continue to worsen. Her shortness of breath occurs mostly during the early morning hours and she has had a hard time for the several months.

The nurse practitioner saw her today, and after discovering that my friend had developed congestive heart failure, it was suggested that **Hospice** be brought in to help look after my friend. She explained that Hospice could give her the extra care she needed at this time in her life. The nurses at the facility were doing a wonderful job, but with the many residents, they were unable to devote a lot of special time to any one person. That is where hospice would come in; they would give her that extra pampering.

Of course this did not sit well with some family members, but from my research about hospice, this was the best thing for her. She would still remain in the facility, so hospice and the facility would collaborate regarding my friend's care.

5

The Last Sibling Gone

When this earthly house of this tabernacle shall be dissolved, we have a building not made by hands eternal in the heavens. *1st Corinthians 5:1* As I reluctantly made my way to my friends room this morning, these are the words that I used to try and comfort her after breaking the news to her that her last sibling had died.

There were many times that she longed to go see her sister who was a resident in another nursing facility, but because of her condition she was unable to make the drive. But somehow God had worked it out, and her sister ended up in the same facility as my friend; their rooms were opposite each other.

From the time she arrived, her sister was in a declining state, and my friend wasn't doing too well herself. My friend was able to visit her sister from time to time, but her sister could not respond to her because she was so sick.

Her sister's stay at the facility was short lived; she refused to eat or drink and rapidly went downhill. Late one evening her sister was transported to the hospital and later that night she went home to be with the Lord.

Carefully the news of her sister's passing was given to my friend. Did she fully comprehend what had been told her, I'm not sure. From the melancholy look on her face, she knew something was going on, but the depth of her understanding could not be apprehended.

The day before her sister was to be put to rest, I mentioned to my friend the date and time and it was if her world had come to an end. She kept saying I didn't know the funeral is tomorrow. I think that talking about the funeral made her sister's passing all too real to her. With tears streaming down her face, it was apparent that she was utterly shaken. As I mentioned earlier, she had been told, but it was evident that she had not realized at that time her sister was gone.

Again the same as I had done when telling my friend her sister was gone, 2nd Corinthians 5:1 was read to her (For we know that if our earthly house of *this* tabernacle were dissolved, we have a building of God, an house not made with hands, eternal in the heavens). I explained to her that as a believer we know and her sister knew by faith that there is another life after this life has ended. Her sister had the good hope through grace that her dwelling place, her resting place and her hiding place was in heaven. Again I told my friend that although her sister was gone in bodily form, she was present with the Lord. This meant no more suffering, no more pain, and no more worries. Her sister had gone to the place that Jesus told his disciples about in John 14, that prepared place.

It didn't take long before God's word took root and had caused my friend to settled down. I began to bellow out the words to an old familiar hymn, "When we all get to Heaven" and afterward left for the day. God's word has a way of calming our spirits and some of the great hymns of the church give us reassurance that everything is going to be alright.

Prayer

Dear God

Thank you for your Holy Word; for when we have no words of our own, in your word we can find just what we need to encourage, strengthen, and comfort your people. When sadness fills the heart, your word says be of good cheer for you dear God have overcome the world. When our strength is weak, your word tells us that your strength is made perfect in weakness. And when in need of comfort, your word tells us not to fear, for you are with us. It tells us to do not be dismayed, for you dear God will strengthen us and will help us. Yes dear God you will uphold us with your righteous right hand. Thank you for the many ways that you give us comfort. You bring comfort through faith, you bring comfort through your word, you bring comfort through others and you bring comfort through me, yes dear God, even me.   Amen

*And the peace of God which passeth all understanding, shall keep your hearts and minds through Christ Jesus. **Philippians 4:7 KJV***

Personal Reflections

Take a moment to write down some of your favorite scriptures that have encouraged you when you were feeling discourage, words that gave you hope when it seemed as if all hope was gone.

_____

_____

_____

_____

_____

_____

_____

_____

_____

_____

Know that the word of God is a lamp unto your feet and a light unto your path. Psalms 119:105. Let the word of God lead you at this difficult time.

What a lovely going home celebration her sister had. So many family and friends gathered together to say their final good-byes. How I wished that my friend could have attended, but there was no way she would have been able to endure. The emotional pressure, coupled with her breathing limitation would have put an enormous amount of strain on her already weakened heart.

I remember a couple of years prior to her sister's passing, my friend was able to gather at the same church for a birthday celebrating. She had gotten her hair done, and on that day she was dressed so pretty. You would have thought she was the birthday girl. How the two sisters enjoyed one another's company on that day. She was able to mingle with all her nieces, nephews, distant cousins and friends.

Although she did not get to attend her sister's funeral services, Hospice however, did a private ceremony with her, a few days after the funeral; what a thoughtful thing to do.

You are at rest now; you have found comfort for your soul
may your rest be sweet knowing that in our
thoughts we will forever hold memories of you
until the mysteries of death shall unfold and we
too shall join with you and all of heaven's best,
after we like you have passed life's final test.

Words by: Reverend Eleanor D. Miller

Behold I show you a mystery: We shall not all sleep;
but we shall all be changed in a moment, in the
*twinkling of an eye…**1ˢᵗ Corinthians 51-52***

Prayer

Dear God I need your help to finish this race called life. Lead me, guide me, and direct my path so that when troubles, adversities and disappointments arise I may stand firm on the fact that you promised never to leave me nor forsake me. As I go from day to day, let me be refreshed by your word which is a lamp to guide my feet and a light for my path. As I follow Christ, the Light of the World, let me illuminate others to the fact that no matter the circumstances, you are with us consoling and strengthening us.

Amen

Another year is just about to come to an end, and it makes three years that my friend has been in the nursing facility. No one thought she would have held on for such a long time with her many health problems, but she has. She has even surprised the Hospice team. A year ago she would experience good days and bad days, but now all she has are bad days. The reality is that she doesn't have too much longer to go. How sad it is to see how she has dwindled away to nothing. Today as I visited her she did not have the energy to get out of bed. She just slept the whole time I was there. If she was conscious, or aware of my presence, she did not make it known.

It seems as late that all my journal entries say the same thing, today is a repeat of the day before or the months before. But as I observe my friend, it only confirms all the things that I have read regarding her condition.

I've read that a person's hearing is the last thing that leaves them, so I sung a hymn or two and afterward sat quietly by her bedside, just in case she awaken; I didn't want her to be alone. Hours had elapsed and she never came around, so I left. Perhaps tomorrow will be better than today is what I told myself as I existed the door.

6

The Ending, Loss of A Friend

For four days I have been unable to visit my friend, because of my dealing with bronchitis. I really missed here, but thought it was best that I stay away. During that four day period, my thoughts were on her constantly. Today I decided to go for a brief visit, just to check on her and see how she was doing. I really wasn't prepared for what I saw.

It was as if her condition had deteriorated in the short time I had been away. I entered her room with anticipation, that once her eyes met mind, a smile would come across her face which was her usual reaction when her eyes met mine, when she was having a good day, but that didn't **happen.** She just had this blank stare on her face. Although there was no response on her part I still talked to her, reminding her that I loved her. Later she went off to sleep.. But it was not a peaceful sleep; she moaned and groaned, a clear sign that she was suffering.

The Hospice nurse had ordered that her morphine be given every hour to help alleviate the pain, this signified to me that her time was drawing near.

Isn't it funny how you know what is happening, but can still be in denial? Is it denial or holding on to a glimmer of hope?

What do you do when you don't know what to do? The answer is pray, and ask God's will to be done. That is what I did.

Lord, not my will, but your will be done in my friend's life. It was the morning of March 14 around 7:30 I got a call from the facility saying my friend had a rough night and now she was making gurgling sounds.

This really didn't sound promising. After getting dressed I went to her bedside, it was bad. Someone said to me, "she's not doing good" never really telling me what was transpiring with my friend.

Minutes later two CNAs came in to clean her up and dress her in a hospital gown. It was suggested that the rest of the family be contacted and so I did.

After the hospice nurse came she reaffirmed what I already knew and said to me that her demise would be today.

I sat with her the entire day. We sang hymns to her just to make her aware she was surrounded by love; not only the love of family and friends, but the love of God. Around

5pm, when another family member came in to relieve me, reluctantly, I went home.

Even though I left her bedside she was still on my mind. I remembered the scripture that says, Isaiah 26:3 Thou wilt keep him in perfect peace whose mind is stayed on thee because he trusteth in thee. That scripture gave me the assurance that whatever happened it would be alright, because I indeed trusted God, therefore I was at peace with whatever God did.

The long expected call came around 3:10 or 3:15 in the early morning hour of March 15th. The person on the phone said she is going, and while the one on the other end was speaking, she said she's gone, she's gone.

After watching my friend for the last two or three days, and seeing how she struggled, I must say that to hear those words, she's gone, were words that moved me to tears. The tears I shed were not tears of sadness, but were tears of joy, for all the pain and suffering that she had endured for ten years was over.

Those ten years were the most debilitating years of her life. Ten years she fought to overcome this disease, but from the onset of her diagnosis, she was told that there was no cure. While there were things that she could do to manage COPD, it would never be cured.

It finally dawned on me why my friend held on as long as she did; it was for me. She knew how devastated I would be when the day she died came. She had been there when my mother passed and had witnessed how sad I was and she did not want to see me suffer through that again. So with everything in her she managed to go just one more day for me. But then when she did not see me for four days, perhaps she felt it was time to let go. I pray that she did not think that I had abandoned her, for I vowed to be there for her no matter what. And I must say, I kept my promise.

What enable me to cope with all that my friend went through, was the knowledge I received from pamphlets and articles that discussed her condition. Also it was my faith in God, and the words I often spoke to my friend, God will not put more on you than you can bear. If I had to do it all over again, I would. For the many hours, and days I sacrificed just to be by her side, did not compare to the joy she brought to my life.

I did what I did not looking for anything in return, but out of a commitment that I made to my friend. I promised her that I would be there for her.

Because I was faithful to her, in the end she was faithful to me; everything she owned in this world, she left it to me. She had made preparations to take care of me at the beginning of our friendship.

She said she would be a mother for me, and just like a mother would do she made sure I was taken care of after she was gone. That's the mystery that William Cowper spoke of in his hymn "Light Shining after darkness". God indeed moves in a mysterious way, His wonders to perform, He plants His footsteps in the sea and rides upon the storm. Through every storm of life or death God is there. And he moves in accordance with the plans He has for our lives.

As events in our lives unfold, we may not fully comprehend, but if we wait until God's plan is complete, things will be made clear.

Romans 8:28 reminds us of this, For we know that all things work together for good to them that love God, to them Who are the called according to His purpose. Sometimes life can be so mysterious, for we cannot see the big picture, but God in His own time reveals everything to us, and puts everything in perspective.

Jesus spoke to his disciples when he washed their feet as recorded in John 13:7 KJV, and said "What I do thou knowest not but thou shalt know hereafter ". Then He told them in verse 14, 15 of the same chapter "If I then, your Lord and Master, have washed your feet, ye also ought to wash one another's feet. For I have given you an example, that ye should do as I have done to you.

I believe Jesus was showing and telling the disciples to be a friend. Be friends to one another and to all who need a friend because I have been a friend to you.

Jesus said if you keep my commands, then you are my friends. And the same way that my friend prepared for me once her life was over, Jesus has prepared a home for us when our time on this side expires. He has prepared an eternal home in heaven.

Because I am a friend of Jesus, I was able to be a friend to my friend.

Forever Friends

It was early one morning my friend
that you slipped away from me.
I knew that time was coming, the day
I had dreaded so long, but despite how lost
I feel I'm glad you are finally free from
the pain and the suffering that
you dealt with so long.
I've cried so many tears, from the sadness I
feel But I know that one day those tears will
turn to tears of joyfulness, because
you have made it to
the place of eternal and lasting rest. I'll
never forget about you, my friend,
nor the life lessons that you taught me.
You showed me how to be a "True Friend"
You were with me to the End.
We will always be, "Forever Friends."

WORK CITIED

Merriam-Webster.com/Thesaurus

biography.com/bio-dorothy-height.html

William Cowper-Wikipedia.org

KJV Bible Copyright © 1976 By Thomas Nelson Inc. Nashville, Tennessee

Printed in the United States
By Bookmasters